THE SUPER SCIENCE
BOOK OF THE
ENVIRONMENT

Sally Morgan
with additional material
by Susan Bullen

GREEN PLACE, GREY PLACE

There is a green place,
Where trees bow their fronds in dappled light
And crystally waters chase fat, brown trout
Over smooth, clay-like pebbles.
Gaudy butterflies dart in and out of dusty sunlight
Spiralling up the glade's gap,
Then hover on emerald blades and catch their breath.

There is a grey place,
Where jagged cans score the velvet pads of rabbits' feet
And the bone-brittle heat grinds the
Barren earth to chalky dust.
Lilies lie face down, suffocating in polluted waters
Reflecting muddy skeletons of trees
Whose leaves have long since choked.

Green place
Grey place
We need our world
To be a green space.

BY LIZZIE LEWIS

Illustrations by Frances Lloyd

Thomson Learning • New York

Books in the Super Science series

Energy	Our Bodies
The Environment	Sound
Forces	Space
Light	Time
Materials	Weather

First published in the United States by
Thomson Learning
115 Fifth Avenue
New York, NY 10003

First published in 1994 by Wayland (Publishers) Ltd.

UK version copyright © 1994 Wayland (Publishers) Ltd.

U.S. version copyright © 1994 Thomson Learning

Green place, grey place copyright © 1993 Liz Lewis

Library of Congress Cataloging-in-Publication Data
Morgan, Sally.
  The super science book of the environment / Sally Morgan
with additional material by Susan Bullen ; illustrations by
Frances Lloyd.
         p.   cm.—(Super science)
  Includes bibliographical references and index.
  ISBN 1-56847-095-9 : $14.95
  1. Environmental sciences—Juvenile literature.
[1. Environmental sciences.] I. Bullen, Susan. II. Lloyd,
Frances, ill. III. Title. IV. Series.
GE115.M67   1994
574.5—dc20   93-41696

Printed in Italy

Series editor: James Kerr
Designer: Loraine Hayes Design

Picture acknowledgments

Illustrations by Frances Lloyd
Cover illustration by Martin Gordon

Photographs by permission of: Bruce Coleman Ltd 29
(above) (Williams), 29 (below) (Krasemann); Ecoscene 6
(Morgan), 8 (Gryniewicz), 9 (Morgan), 11 (Blowfield), 13
(Platt), 15 (above) (Harwood), 15 (below) (Morgan), 17
(above) (Kloske), 17 (below) (Rout), 19 (above) (Brown), 19
(below) (Schaffer), 21, 22 (Morgan), 23 (both) (Morgan), 25
(above) (Morgan), 26 (above) (Harwood), 26 (below)
(Morgan); Energy Technology Visuals Collection 13; Mary
Evans Picture Library 7; Wayland 7; ZEFA 25 (below)
(Heilman).

CONTENTS

OUR ENVIRONMENT

Wherever you go, whatever you do, the environment is all around you. It includes living things, such as plants and animals, and nonliving things, such as soil, rocks, water, and air.

Living things arc in the air, on and just below earth's surface, and in the water. This narrow band containing all living things on our planet is called the biosphere. Everything in the biosphere is finely balanced. Plants, animals, and virtually all living things take in oxygen and give off carbon dioxide. But, during the day, plants also absorb carbon dioxide and give off oxygen as part of a special food-making process. Plants give off more oxygen then they take in. This oxygen that plants give off helps to maintain the balance of carbon dioxide and oxygen in the air.

This balance can easily be upset by human actions. If we cut down too many trees, for example, there may be too much carbon dioxide left in the atmosphere. Everything we do affects our environment. And every change in our environment affects all living things.

Australian Aborigines have a close relationship with the environment. Each Aborigine has a particular link to one animal or plant, and will try not to harm it. He or she feels traditionally that this animal or plant is linked with his or her own fate. Each person also has a special place linked to where he or she was born.

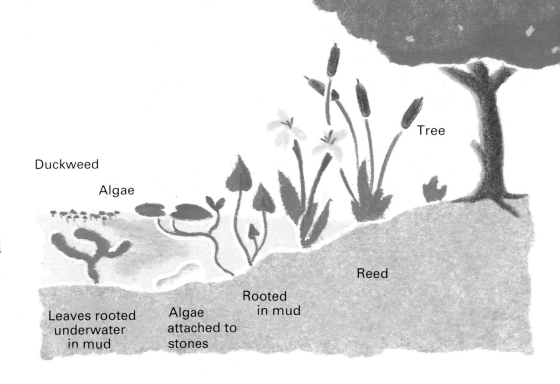

Duckweed

Algae

Tree

Reed

Rooted in mud

Leaves rooted underwater in mud

Algae attached to stones

The place where a plant or animal ▲ lives is called its habitat. This pond is a habitat with a large community of plants and animals. It offers plenty of food and places to live.

A small habitat, such as a pond, may be part of a larger habitat, such as a forest. If the pond gradually dried up, the forest would be affected. Water-loving trees would find it hard to survive without the pond. But oaks could grow in their place. All habitats are linked in some way.

Describe a Habitat

1 Think of a habitat you know well (such as a pond, woodland, or city dump).
2 Write about the wildlife there.
3 Imagine you revisit the habitat in five years and it has changed. For example, a road has been built. How would you react to the changes? How would they affect the environment?

THE CHANGING ENVIRONMENT

Look at yourself. Have you changed in the last five years? All living things change. Sometimes changes happen quickly; sometimes they take millions of years.

This tree is growing in a windy place. ▶ It does not grow tall and straight. Instead, the branches grow only on the sheltered side, producing a lopsided shape. The tree's shape changes as an effect of the the wind.

Habitats change over time. A pond eventually becomes clogged with plants and mud, and a bog forms. As the ground dries out, trees start to grow where there was once a pond. Animals that like water are replaced by those that prefer dry land.

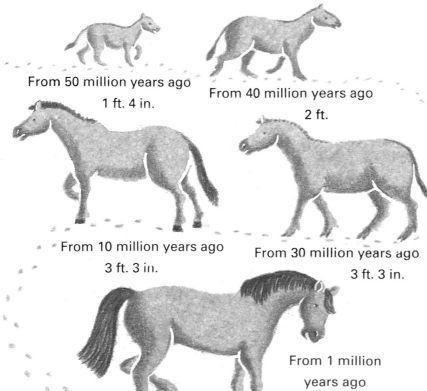

From 50 million years ago
1 ft. 4 in.

From 40 million years ago
2 ft.

From 10 million years ago
3 ft. 3 in.

From 30 million years ago
3 ft. 3 in.

From 1 million years ago
5 ft. 3 in.

◀ Animals and plants adapt to their evolving environment over a very long time. Fifty million years ago, horses were small animals with four toes, and they lived in forests. As the climate changed, their wooded habitats became grassland. Horses became taller and faster to escape their predators on the open grasslands. Their teeth changed so that they could eat tough grasses.

People have been changing their surroundings for thousands of years. Early peoples cleared land for farming. The ancient Greeks and Romans built cities, roads, and bridges more than 2,000 years ago.

The natural environment changes slowly over time but is almost always in balance. If changes caused by humans happen too quickly, the balance can be upset.

◀ In the nineteenth century, people began to change the environment on a large scale. Many factories were built. These pumped thick, black smoke from their chimneys, causing air pollution.

However, some harmful ▶ changes are caused by natural events. An erupting volcano pumps sulfur dioxide into the air. This gas mixes with moisture in the air, making acid rain. In fact, dust and gases from volcanoes can cause the world climate to change for a short time.

Hot ash and gases (containing sulfur dioxide)

Crater

Lava

Rock

Vent

CYCLES OF LIFE

The living world changes constantly. ▶ Hundreds of aphids are born on a rosebush, while elsewhere hundreds of other aphids are eaten by hungry ladybugs. A dead tree rots into the ground, but its nutrients enrich the soil for future trees. These cycles of life go on all the time. They keep the living world in balance.

All the millions of different plants and animals on our planet contain the elements carbon, hydrogen, oxygen, and nitrogen, which are also found in various combinations in air, soil, and water. If these vital elements could be used only once, they would soon run out.

Fortunately, nearly everything can be reused. There are many cycles in the biosphere – for example, the carbon cycle, the nitrogen cycle, and the water cycle. They are all interlinked in some way.

Water is in a continuous cycle – a chain of events involving all parts of the biosphere. The sun heats water in seas, lakes, and rivers. The water turns into vapor (evaporates) and rises into the air. Here the water vapor cools and condenses into clouds of droplets. These fall as rain on land and sea, and then the cycle begins again. ▼

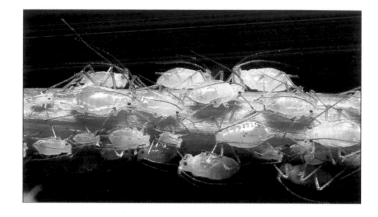

Snow and rainfall

Water vapor condenses

Woodland

Water evaporates from the sea

Water evaporates from trees and land

Streams and rivers flow to the sea

Sea

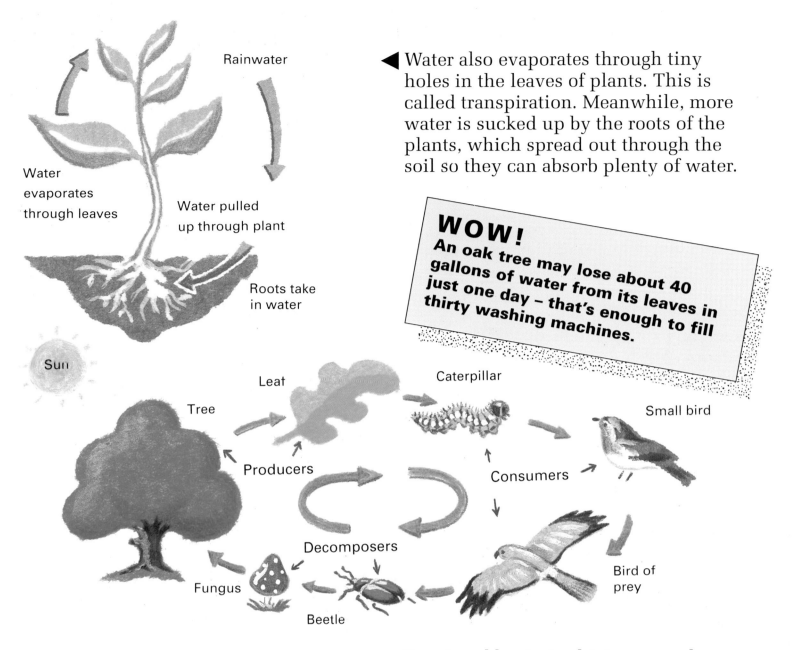

Rainwater

Water evaporates through leaves

Water pulled up through plant

Roots take in water

Sun

◀ Water also evaporates through tiny holes in the leaves of plants. This is called transpiration. Meanwhile, more water is sucked up by the roots of the plants, which spread out through the soil so they can absorb plenty of water.

WOW!
An oak tree may lose about 40 gallons of water from its leaves in just one day – that's enough to fill thirty washing machines.

Leaf

Tree

Producers

Caterpillar

Small bird

Consumers

Decomposers

Bird of prey

Fungus

Beetle

The food chain is another important ▲ cycle. It is a cycle of energy that starts with the sun. Green plants make their own food using the sun's energy. We call them producers.

Animals cannot make their own food. They must consume (eat) plants or other animals to get energy, so they are called consumers. Plant-eating animals, like rabbits, deer, and sheep, are called herbivores. They are eaten by carnivores – meat-eating animals such as foxes, lions, and eagles.

Fungi and bacteria obtain energy by breaking down dead plant and animal matter. We call them decomposers. They return the nutrients that make plants grow to the soil. The food chain is a complete cycle. ▼

POPULATIONS

How many elephants are there in the world…and how many ants? No one knows the exact number. The populations of these animals change all the time as new animals are born and others die.

In the summer, look at some rosebushes in your garden or in a park. How many aphids can you spot? How many ladybugs can you see?

Ladybugs feed on aphids. If there are plenty of aphids, the ladybugs have lots of food and will breed, making more ladybugs.

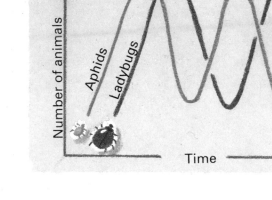
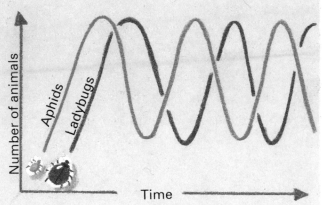

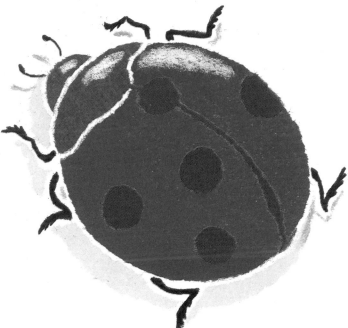

▲ The graph shows how changes in the aphid population affect the number of ladybugs. When there are not enough aphids to go around, some ladybugs go hungry and their population starts to decrease. When there are fewer ladybugs, more aphids survive and the aphid population starts to increase. This then leads to an increase in the ladybug population.

So the sizes of the ladybug and aphid populations are linked.

Grow Duckweed

Duckweed is a tiny green plant that grows quickly over the surface of ponds and lakes.

1 Take a single piece of duckweed and place it in a small container of pond water.

2 Leave it on a window-sill for a few months, adding a little pond water when needed.

3 Once a week, count the number of duckweed leaves.

4 Plot a graph to show the increase in leaves.

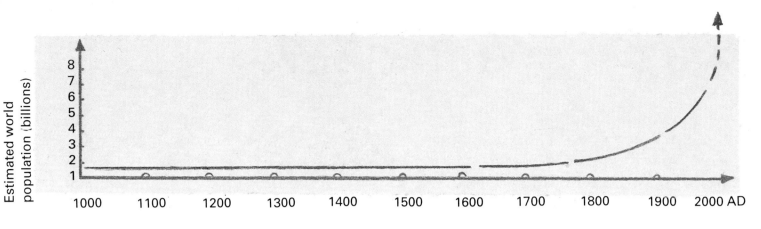

Estimated world population (billions)

8
7
6
5
4
3
2
1

1000 1100 1200 1300 1400 1500 1600 1700 1800 1900 2000 AD

▲ This graph shows how the human population has grown over the last thousand years. The steep line on the right-hand side tells us that the human population is increasing very fast.

Two thousand years ago there were fewer than 100 million people living on earth. Today there are more than five billion. Imagine how crowded the world could be twenty years from now!

▲ The human population is rising fast, but our numbers are still cut down by disease and food shortages. In some developing countries, millions of people die because they do not have enough food or water, or because they catch diseases like typhoid, diarrhea, or malaria. Now, all over the world, people face a new threat from AIDS.

WOW!
Every minute of every day, about 200 babies are born around the world.

ENERGY

What happens to you when you walk, run, swim, or ride a bicycle? You use energy. And where does this energy come from? From your food – food is fuel for your body.

We also need energy to run our cars, generate electricity for our homes, and drive industry. We get this energy by burning fossil fuels such as coal, oil, and gas. These fuels are the fossil remains of plants and animals that died millions of years ago. When we burn them, we release the energy that the animals absorbed from food and the plants absorbed from the sun when they were alive. ▼

Fossil fuels are called nonrenewable sources of energy. We can use them only once, and today we are using them up very quickly. There may be enough coal to last until the year 2240, but some scientists believe supplies of oil and gas will probably run out in the next fifty years. Remember: there are more than five billion people in the world.

Luckily, there are other sources of energy that will not run out. We can use the energy from wind, sunlight, ocean waves, and mountain rivers. These renewable energy sources are mostly nonpolluting, although it takes expensive technology to be able to use their energy on a large scale.

◀ In California there are huge wind farms that turn wind energy into electricity. The wind turns the angled blades of turbines, and these drive a generator for producing electricity. A wind turbine is a modern type of windmill. Some people don't like wind turbines because they think they make the landscape look ugly.

Solar power plants use solar panels ▶ to change energy from the sun's rays into hot water and then electricity. But it takes many solar panels to generate enough electricity for a small city.

Some houses have heat-absorbing solar panels on the roof. The sun's warmth heats up water that runs through pipes inside the panels, and this hot water can then be used for washing or cleaning in the home.

WOW!
The sun could provide the world's energy requirements for a whole year in just thirty minutes – but first we must find a way to control all of the sun's energy so that we can use it.

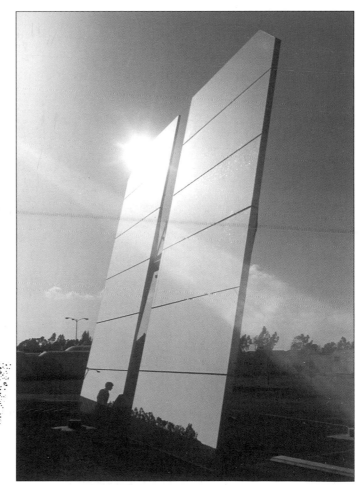

RECYCLING

Think of all the leaves that fall from deciduous trees every autumn. Why don't we see piles of them six months later? They are quickly broken down by nature's waste disposal experts – by decomposers such as bacteria and fungi. The nutrients from the leaves are returned to the soil and are used again.

Every day we throw away a lot of garbage. Some of the things we throw away – such as paper, food, and natural cloth rags – will rot. These things are biodegradable. However, some materials, such as plastic, will never rot. The elements they contain can be reused only if humans recycle them.

Find out Which Materials are Biodegradable

1 In your garden or school field, dig four holes, each 4 inches deep.

2 Put an apple core in one hole, a lettuce leaf in the second, a small plastic bag in the third, and a foam (polystyrene) cup in the fourth.

3 Write the name of each item on a small piece of cardboard and staple this to a stick. Place each stick in the ground by the hole, matching the label to the buried item.

4 Cover each hole with soil.

5 One month later, go back to your holes and dig up the four items. What has happened to each item? Which are biodegradable?

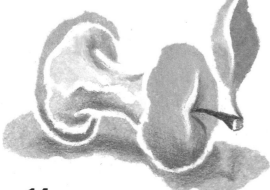

◄ Most of our household garbage is taken to landfills, where it is buried in holes in the ground. But the glass, plastic, metal, paper, and cloth we throw away can be recycled. Today, most towns and cities have recycling stations where you can take your waste. Do you recycle anything?

Metals can be collected, heated in ► ovens so that they melt, and then reshaped into new items. The aluminum that is used to make drink cans can be recycled over and over, saving resources and energy and reducing waste. However, it still takes some energy to transport the old metal cans to the recycling plant and to produce the heat to melt the metals.

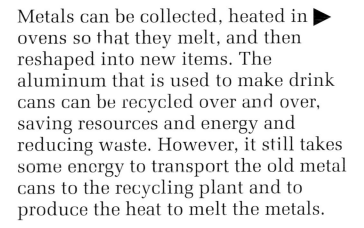

WOW!
It takes twenty times more energy to make one new aluminum can from the raw material – bauxite – than it does to make one from old cans.

WATER FOR ALL?

All living things need water to survive. The world appears to have plenty of water: water covers 70 percent of the earth's surface. But less than 1 percent is the fresh water in rivers and lakes that is needed by most plants and animals. The rest is either frozen at the South and North Poles or is saltwater in the oceans. ▼

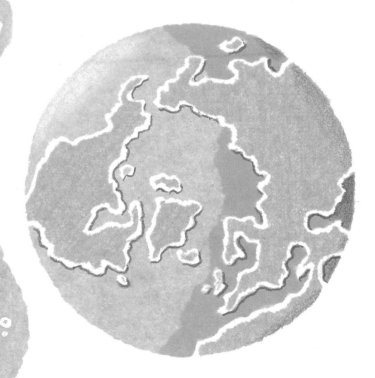

Water is a precious resource, but our modern way of life means that we use more and more of it. Just think how often you and the people you live with use water for washing, cooking, or cleaning, or how often you flush water down the toilet.

Some of this dirty water is cleaned in the sewage system so that it can be used again. But a lot of water goes to waste, too. Many countries suffer droughts, when water is in short supply, and people have to try to use it more carefully.

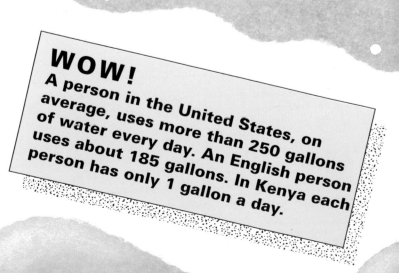

WOW!
A person in the United States, on average, uses more than 250 gallons of water every day. An English person uses about 185 gallons. In Kenya each person has only 1 gallon a day.

◄ Reservoirs store water for irrigating crops or to supply cities with drinking water. People make reservoirs by building a strong dam across a big river. The water is held back and gradually forms a lake. The immense power of this stored water can be used to turn turbines and generate electricity. But sometimes a reservoir floods a valley and its villages and natural habitats. (Notice the trees sticking out of the water in this photograph.) The river below a dam carries less water than it did originally, and this affects the river's wildlife.

We use rivers, lakes, and oceans as sewers and as dumping grounds for waste and polluted water. Waste dumped into running water is quickly carried away out of sight. However, if too much waste is dumped into water, nothing can live in it.

◄ Why is this river bright green? It is covered by a thick, slimy blanket of tiny plants called algae. This is a sign that the river is polluted, because algae grow very fast when water contains sewage and artificial fertilizers. When the algae die, millions of bacteria break down the algae and use up the oxygen in the water, so fish suffocate.

THE **AIR** AROUND US

The air we breathe is made up of a number of gases. It consists mostly of nitrogen, with some oxygen and a little carbon dioxide. All these gases are essential to living things. Fortunately, they are constantly recycled. All parts of the biosphere are involved in these cycles of nitrogen, oxygen, and carbon.

If these cycles are balanced, the amounts of gases in the air we breathe will stay the same. Plants use up carbon dioxide and produce oxygen. Animals use up oxygen and produce carbon dioxide. As animals absorb oxygen, plants replace it, so the amount of oxygen in the air stays the same.

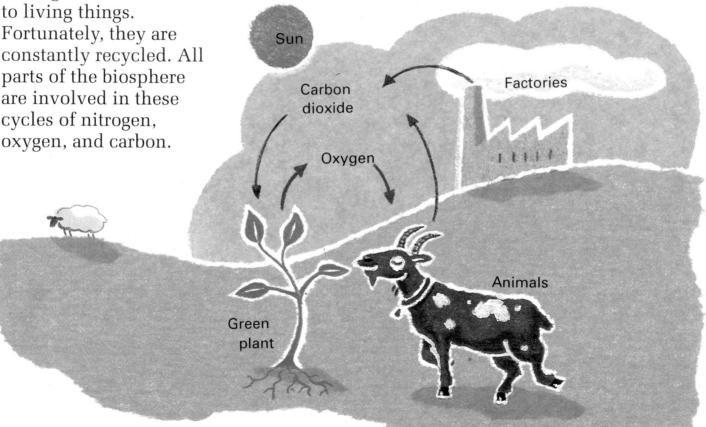

Sun

Carbon dioxide

Factories

Oxygen

Green plant

Animals

When fossil fuels are burned, oxygen is used up and carbon dioxide is produced. The level of carbon dioxide in the air is increasing because we are using so much fossil fuel. If the amounts of gases in the air we breathe change too much, the natural balance of gases will be upset.

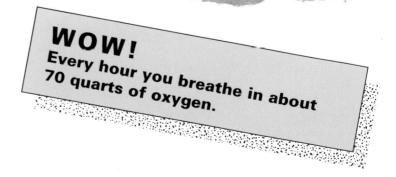

WOW!
Every hour you breathe in about 70 quarts of oxygen.

See the Effect of Acid on Plants

1 Place some cotton in three small plastic tubs with drainage holes in the bottom. Label the three tubs "strong acid," "weak acid," and "water."
2 Label three one-quart plastic bottles in the same way.
3 Fill the bottle marked "water" with tap water; put half a pint of vinegar in the "weak acid" bottle and fill it up with water; put a little more than a pint of vinegar in the "strong acid" bottle and fill it up with water.
4 Pour a little liquid from the correct bottle into each tub, so that the cotton is moist but not waterlogged.
5 Sprinkle cress seeds over the moist cotton.
6 Water the seeds daily, using the correct bottle and the same amount of liquid for each tub.
7 Check the plants' appearance. Can you spot any differences?

Air is precious. Without it, we would die within minutes. Clean air has no smell or color, but polluted air contains harmful gases or particles of soot and dust.

◀ Sometimes a gray-green haze called smog builds up in the air above a city. Los Angeles and Mexico City suffer from heavy smog, caused mainly by car exhaust gases.

Acid rain forms when the gases sulfur dioxide and nitrogen oxide, from industry and car exhausts, react with water droplets in the air. Acid rain has killed some of these conifer trees in Germany. It also harms wildlife in lakes and eats away at stone buildings. ▼

GASES IN THE ATMOSPHERE

The earth is surrounded by a layer of gases called the atmosphere. High in the atmosphere there is a layer of ozone about 15 miles thick. Ozone is a form of oxygen that blocks the sun's harmful ultraviolet rays so that they don't reach earth.

Too much ultraviolet light is harmful to people, causing skin cancers and eye disorders. It can also harm plankton in the sea and damage the eggs of fish and crustaceans, such as crabs and lobsters.

As long as there is plenty of ozone, the earth is protected. In recent years, however, the ozone layer has become much thinner, especially over Antarctica. The damage is mostly caused by chemicals called CFCs (chlorofluorocarbons) that come from aerosols, refrigerators, polystyrene packaging, and industrial processes.

The CFCs rise high into the atmosphere, where they stay for up to 130 years. The ultraviolet light from the sun breaks down the CFCs, releasing a gas called chlorine. This gas attacks and destroys the protective ozone, so ultraviolet rays can get through to earth. ▼

WOW!
A single CFC molecule can destroy up to 100,000 ozone molecules.

Ionosphere

Stratosphere containing ozone layer

Troposphere

Ultraviolet sunlight

Antarctica

Some of the gases in ▶ the atmosphere act like a greenhouse. They let light and heat from the sun into the atmosphere and keep heat from escaping. Without them, the earth would be too cold for life.

Greenhouse gas	Percentage contribution to the greenhouse effect
Carbon dioxide	50
Methane	18
CFCs	14
Ozone, low level	12
Nitrous oxide	6

◀ Methane is released by rotting vegetation in swampy areas such as rice paddies. It is also released when grazing cattle break wind. A single cow can give off 77,000 quarts of methane every year — enough to fill a hot-air balloon.

Everybody breathes out carbon ▶ dioxide, another greenhouse gas. But it also pours into the atmosphere when people burn down forests or burn fuel in factories, power plants, and cars. As more and more greenhouse gases are produced, more heat is trapped in the atmosphere. Some scientists think this is making the atmosphere and the earth gradually warm up. We call this the greenhouse effect.

If the global temperature rises by just a few degrees Fahrenheit, there will be a big change in the world climate. Some of the ice at the North and South Poles would melt, causing the level of the water in the oceans to rise. Low-lying land would be flooded, and some islands might disappear altogether!

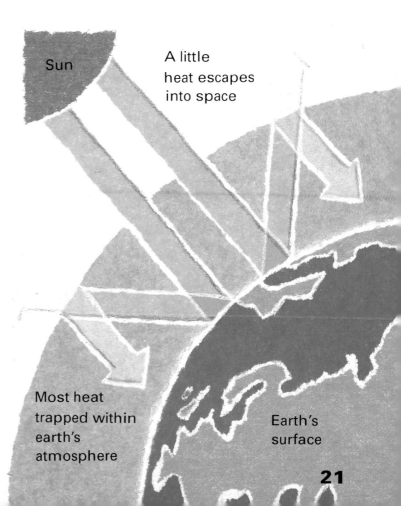

Sun

A little heat escapes into space

Most heat trapped within earth's atmosphere

Earth's surface

TREES FOR LIFE

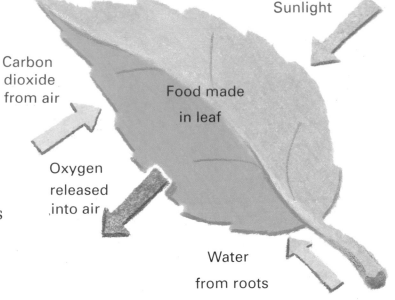

Sunlight

Carbon dioxide from air

Food made in leaf

Oxygen released into air

Water from roots

We owe a lot to trees. Their wood is used all over the world as a fuel, as a building material, and as paper. Trees are home to many hundreds of animals and plants, from algae to tropical orchids that grow on the bark of some trees.

Trees absorb carbon dioxide from the atmosphere and use it to make starch for food. This process is called photosynthesis. If we keep planting trees and protecting large forests, ▲ more carbon dioxide will be absorbed and this will help to combat the greenhouse effect.

▲ Some of the largest forests in the world are the tropical rain forests of South America, central Africa, Southeast Asia and northeast Australia. They are home to the greatest variety of plants and animals on earth. Many tribal people live in rain forests, too. For many years they have found all their needs in these forests and have lived in harmony with nature.

22

Today, over half of the world's ▲ rain forests have been burned or cut down. People want the quality timber from rain forest trees. They also need space to grow crops or to graze cattle. As these vast forests burn, huge amounts of carbon dioxide pour into the atmosphere, adding to the greenhouse effect.

Did you know that many of our foods and medicines originate from rain forests? They include coffee, tea, cocoa, bananas, yams, and the anti-malaria drug, quinine. Unless we act soon to save rain forests, we will lose many new foods and medicinal plants even before we know their value.

WOW!
More than 1,000 animal species live in any one oak tree.

A group of giant rain forest trees acts like a sponge, holding large amounts of water. Look back at pages 8 and 9 to see how this process works. When the forests are cleared, the water runs straight off the land into rivers and is carried out to sea. Precious soil is washed away, too.

▲ In North America, conifer forests are being cleared for timber and paper. Some of the forests are replanted, but the new forests are not nearly as rich and varied in animal and plant life as the original forests.

LIVING SOIL

Soil is made up of lots of minute ▶ particles. As well as tiny bits of rock, there are remains of dead plants and animals, called humus. Humus adds nutrients to the soil. Air and water fill the spaces between the particles.

Find the Animals in Soil

1 Collect a large handful of leaf litter and soil from under a tree and put it in a bucket.
2 Tip a little onto a sheet of paper.
3 With a magnifying glass, look carefully at the many small animals that feed on the leaves. The leaves become part of the soil as they are broken down. You may see a few predators, such as centipedes and spiders. They eat the smaller animals.

False scorpion

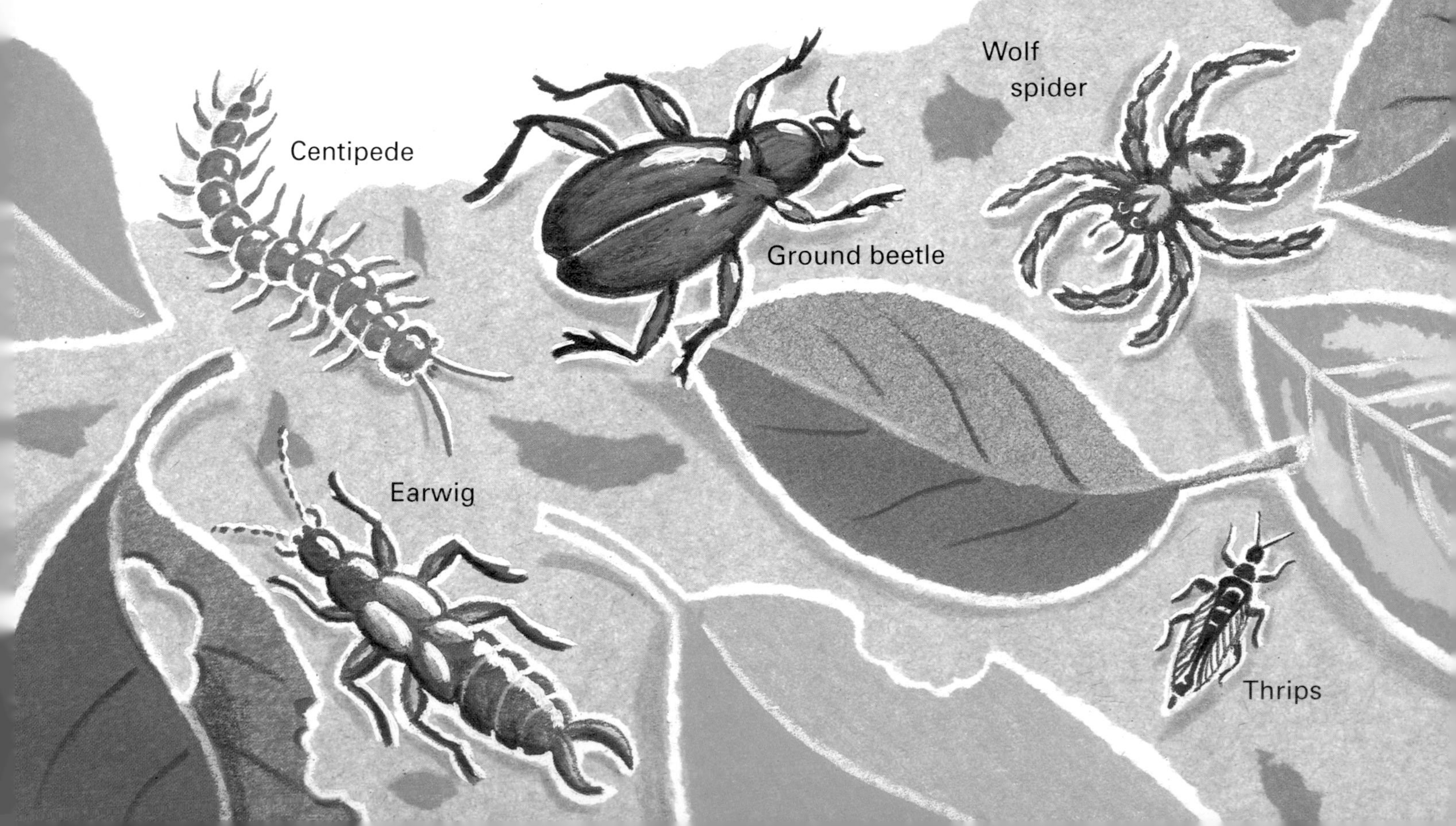

Wolf spider

Centipede

Ground beetle

Earwig

Thrips

◀ Soil takes a very long time to form, but it can be lost in just a few years. When many trees are cut down, there are no roots to bind the soil particles together, and no fallen leaves to protect the soil from the rain. The unprotected soil is swept away by winds and water. This is called soil erosion.

Soil erosion can also occur when farmers allow too many animals to graze on poor grassland. As the ground loses its protective covering of plants, the soil dries up and blows away, leaving bare patches of ground.

Hundreds of years ago, farmers grew ▶ different crops in small fields. As some crops took nutrients out of the soil, others enriched it again. A modern type of farming, called monoculture, upsets the natural cycles. The nutrients are taken from the soil by a single type of crop, year after year. Gradually, the soil loses its goodness, so the farmer adds artificial chemicals – called fertilizers – to keep the soil fertile.

WOW!
It may take 1,000 years for rock to break down into small particles and form a layer of soil just one inch deep.

DISAPPEARING HABITATS

As the human population increases, we need more space for homes, farmland, and industry. We need to dig up more resources. All this destroys natural habitats, from rain forests to flower meadows.

This housing development is taking ▶ up heathland – a habitat of heather, gorse, and pine and birch trees that used to cover much of southern England and northern Germany. Today, just a few fragments remain. But heathland itself was encouraged to grow when people cut and burned down natural forests many hundreds of years ago.

Balancing human need for natural resources with animals' and plants' needs for natural habitats is not easy. Laws that protect valuable wildlife habitats have been passed. Building, farming, and industry must take place in other areas. Whether this continues depends on what future human beings decide to allow other species.

◀ Coal is a valuable resource. In Germany and other countries coal is stripped from large opencast mines by huge machines. The landscape that is left looks like something from a science fiction movie. Prompt replanting of mined areas helps to lessen soil damage.

The Cherokee Indians of North America believed that all things had a spirit and should be treated with respect. Animals and trees were their brothers and sisters. They believed that people belonged to the land – land did not belong to people. In 1855, Chief Seattle said:

Man did not weave the web of life; he is merely a strand in it. Whatever he does to the web he does to himself.

Sometimes a plant or animal species dies out naturally. This happens if there is a dramatic change of climate, for example. Some scientists think this is what happened to the dinosaurs, many millions of years ago.

But many species have died out as a result of human activity, usually hunting. Today, animal species such as certain whales and the snow leopard are threatened by hunting. But the biggest threat to wildlife is habitat loss. This danger is facing majestic animals such as the giant panda, the mountain gorilla, and the tiger. It will take a great deal of human effort to save them. ▼

WOW!
When a single plant species becomes extinct, up to forty animal species that depended on it may also be threatened.

THE VARIETY OF LIFE

No one is sure how many different species of plants and animals live on earth. Scientists have identified more than one million, but there may be more than 10 million more. The existence of such a great range of species is called biodiversity.

Plants provide us with building materials, fibers for fabrics and paper, and many different foods, such as cereals, fruits, nuts, and vegetables. Some plants, many of which come from rain forests, provide us with medicines.

Animals and plants are just as important as coal or oil. It is vital to keep as many species alive as possible. All the flowers in our gardens and the fruit and vegetables we eat were originally bred from wild plants.

In the future, these crops may not be suited to a different climate or to curing new diseases. Then we will need wild plants to help us to breed different crops for the new environment.

WOW!
There are more than 20,000 species of edible plants in the world, but we eat only 3,000.

African hunting dog

Wild dog rose

Poodle

Garden rose

As people have realized the dangers facing plants and animals, they have begun to help them. Sometimes the only way to keep a species from becoming extinct is to protect and breed individual animals in zoos. Then one day they can be released back into the wild.

For example, the coastal rain forest ▶ habitat of a South American monkey called the golden lion tamarin was being cut down. Some monkeys were specially bred in London Zoo, and now they have been put back in a small part of their natural environment.

▲ In the 1950s, fewer than thirty of these Hawaiian nene geese were left in their natural habitat. Three birds were taken to Britain to be bred in captivity. By 1978, hundreds of birds had been bred. They were taken to Hawaii and released into the wild. Scientists are tracking how well the geese are adapting.

We can also protect rare species with laws, but these are not easy to enforce. The best way to conserve wildlife is to protect their habitats as nature preserves — areas of land where plants and animals can live in peace.

There are now many preserves all over the world, from rain forests to snowy mountaintops. They show us that people can do good things to help the plants and animals that share this planet with us.

GLOSSARY

Acid rain   An acidic mixture of rainwater and gases. It can harm trees, lakes, and buildings.

Atmosphere   The layer of gases around the earth.

Atom   The smallest part of an element.

Bacteria   Tiny living things consisting of one cell.

Biodegradable   Able to be broken down by biological means.

Biosphere   That part of the earth (air, land, and water) that contains all living things.

CFCs   Chloroflourocarbons. Harmful chemicals that harm the ozone. In the United States and some other countries, the use of CFCs in many products has been banned. However, the ban is not worldwide and CFCs will remain in the ozone for many years.

Conifers   Evergreen trees and shrubs.

Conserve   To protect wildlife and habitats.

Cycle   A series of events that repeat themselves in a loop.

Deciduous   Trees that lose all their leaves every winter.

Element   A naturally occurring substance whose atoms are all the same kind.

Erosion   The wearing away of land and soil by the action of wind and water.

Extinct   When all individuals of a species have died out.

Fertile   Having nutrients that will allow plenty of plants to grow.

Fertilizers   Chemicals that are put in soil and on crops to make them grow faster and bigger.

Food chain   A cycle in which food energy is passed from the earth to plants, then to animals that eat plants, and then to animals that eat other animals.

Fungi   Living creatures that are not animals or plants. They live on other living things.

Greenhouse effect   The trapping of heat near the surface of the earth by gases, chiefly carbon dioxide, in the atmosphere. The gases act like the glass or plastic roof of a greenhouse, making the harmful rays of the sun stronger. This could result in an increase in the earth's temperature.

Habitat   The place where a plant, animal, or other living thing lives.

Humus   The remains of dead plants and animals. Humus nourishes soil.

Landfill   A large hole where waste is dumped. When full, the site is covered with soil.

Molecule   The smallest unit of a chemical compound. It usually consists of a group of atoms.

Monoculture   The cultivation of the same crop for many years, often over a large area.

Nutrient   Something that provides food for a plant or animal.

Pollution   Harm done to the natural environment, for example by dumping waste at sea.

Predators   Animals that hunt and eat other animals. They can be large or small.

Recycling   Making something from a waste product, rather than using raw materials.

Resources   Natural things we can use, such as water, wind, minerals, timber, and food plants.

Smog   A very dense, dirty fog caused by exhaust or smoke.

Species   A single type of animal or plant.

Transpiration   The evaporation of water from tiny openings in leaves.

Tropical   Situated on or near the equator. These areas have a warm, moist climate.

Turbine   A machine with blades that rotate and release energy.

Ultraviolet light   A type of light that we cannot see. It can tan and burn skin.

Vapor   Moisture in the air.

BOOKS TO READ

Baines, John. *Environmental Disasters.* World's Disasters. New York: Thomson Learning, 1993.

Bennett, Paul. *Earth: The Incredible Recycling Machine.* New York: Thomson Learning, 1993.

Earthworks Group Staff. *Kid Heroes of the Environment: Simple Things Real Kids Are Doing To Save the Earth.* Berkeley, CA: Earth Works, 1991.

Goldberg, Jake. *Economics and the Environment.* New York: Chelsea House, 1993.

Harris, Colin. *Protecting the Planet.* Young Geographer. New York: Thomson Learning, 1993.

Liptak, Karen. *Saving Our Wetlands and Their Wildlife.* First Books. New York: Franklin Watts, 1991.

Peckham, Alexander. *Global Warming.* Issues. New York: Gloucester Press, 1991.

Stidworthy, John. *Environmentalist.* Be an Expert. New York: Gloucester Press, 1992.

Wong, Ovid. *Hands-On Ecology.* Science Activities. Chicago: Children's Press, 1991.

Zeff, Robin L. *Environmental Action Groups.* New York: Chelsea House, 1993.

INDEX